from SmarterComics

MACHIAVELLI

from SmarterComics

# MACHIAVELLI

| | |
|---|---|
| Cullen Bunn | Script Consultant |
| Brian J. Flores | Editor |
| Jennifer Kunz | Creative Director |
| Sander Pieterse | Media Designer |
| Franco Arda | CEO SmarterComics |

ISBN: 978-1-61082-003-5



The Graphic Novel version is based on Nicolo Machiavelli's The Prince, translated by W.K. Marriott.

Printed in Canada

# Introduction

**What is it about POWER that fascinates us so?**

Human beings are captivated by the allure and the art of power. How we can achieve it? How we can keep it?

For many—especially for those who are not in power—it can seem that the only way to attain greatness is to lie, cheat, and steal. Does that mean you must sacrifice your own sense of morality if you are ever going to take what is rightfully yours? Must you become ruthless if you have any hope of keeping your throne?

No wonder Niccolo Machiavelli's masterpiece on the subject of power—THE PRINCE—has become one of the most influential books in the history of the world. Considered by many to be one of the first published works of modern political philosophy, THE PRINCE is a treatise on glory, survival, and ethics that has influenced businessmen, conquerors, and kings.

Published in 1532, THE PRINCE has been a guiding book on the art of power for centuries. Used not only by politicians, but also by anyone who needs to struggle to attain control of people or situations—whether a student, athlete, business person, or parent. These guidelines have withstood the test of time because of Machiavelli's deep understanding on the manipulation and exercise of power.

The pursuit of power requires more than a cunning mind and an ability to outmaneuver your enemies. Machiavelli understood that there was a price—a human toll—to success. Becoming a "prince" isn't necessarily going to make you popular, but it will make you powerful. In the realm of kings, friendship is a luxury, strategy is a necessity, and the fear of losing your grip is a constant companion. It may be good to be the King, but it's never easy.

*Your SmarterComics team*

IT'S BETTER TO BE FEARED THAN LOVED,
IF YOU CANNOT BE BOTH.

HOW MANY KINDS OF PRINCIPALITIES THERE ARE...

...AND BY WHAT MEANS THEY ARE ACQUIRED

PRINCIPALITIES ARE EITHER HEREDITARY, IN WHICH THE FAMILY HAS BEEN LONG ESTABLISHED, OR THEY ARE NEW.

THE NEW ARE EITHER ENTIRELY NEW OR THEY ARE MEMBERS ANNEXED TO THE HEREDITARY STATE OF THE PRINCE WHO HAS ACQUIRED THEM.

SUCH DOMINIONS THUS ACQUIRED ARE EITHER ACCUSTOMED TO LIVING UNDER A PRINCE, OR TO LIVING IN FREEDOM.

THEY ARE ACQUIRED EITHER BY THE ARMS OF THE PRINCE HIMSELF, OR OF OTHERS, OR ELSE BY FORTUNE OR BY ABILITY.

HEY, MR.
KIRBY...

SHOESHINE?
SURE, JOHNNY.

# the Prince

THERE IS NO AVOIDING WAR; IT CAN ONLY BE POSTPONED TO THE ADVANTAGE OF OTHERS.

...HAVE HAD THEIR BIRTH AND BEGINNING IN BASENESS AND OBSCURITY...

...OR HAVE BEEN AGGRIEVED BY FORTUNE IN SOME OUTRAGEOUS WAY.

THEY HAVE EITHER BEEN EXPOSED TO THE MERCY OF WILD BEASTS...

WOOF!

WOOF!

SKIT

...OR THEY HAVE HAD SO MEAN A PARENTAGE THAT IN SHAME THEY HAVE GIVEN THEMSELVES OUT TO BE SONS OF JOVE OR OF SOME OTHER DEITY.

I BELIEVE THAT THESE LOWLY BEGINNINGS OCCUR BECAUSE FORTUNE IS DESIROUS OF SHOWING THE WORLD THAT SUCH MEN OWE MUCH TO HER...

ROXIE!

...AND LITTLE TO WISDOM.

OKAERI!

...BECAUSE SHE BEGINS TO SHOW HER HAND WHEN WISDOM CAN REALLY TAKE NO PART IN THEIR CAREER.

BUT SHE STILL LEAVES US TO DIRECT THE OTHER HALF...

PROGRESS...

...AND HE WHO HAS RELIED LEAST ON FORTUNE...

OR...

...IF THE MAN BE RICH LET HIM EAT WHEN HE IS HUNGRY; IF HE BE POOR, THEN WHEN HE CAN...
...I'M SAYIN' THE SHIT ON THE GOLDEN MENU IS JUST BETTER.
...AND TO THE PRINCE WHO GOES FORTH WITH HIS ARMY, SUPPORTING IT BY PILLAGE, SACK, AND EXTORTION, HANDLING THAT WHICH BELONGS TO OTHERS...
COUGH
WAY BETTER THAN GWAI LO MEIN.
...THIS LIBERALITY IS NECESSARY.
AND OF THAT WHICH IS NEITHER YOURS NOR YOUR SUBJECTS' YOU CAN BE A READY GIVER...
WHAT?!
...BECAUSE IT DOES NOT TAKE AWAY YOUR REPUTATION IF YOU SQUANDER THAT OF OTHERS...
...BUT ADDS TO IT.
YOU SKIP SCHOOL AGAIN?
NO.
IT IS ONLY SQUANDERING YOUR OWN THAT INJURES YOU.

NO.
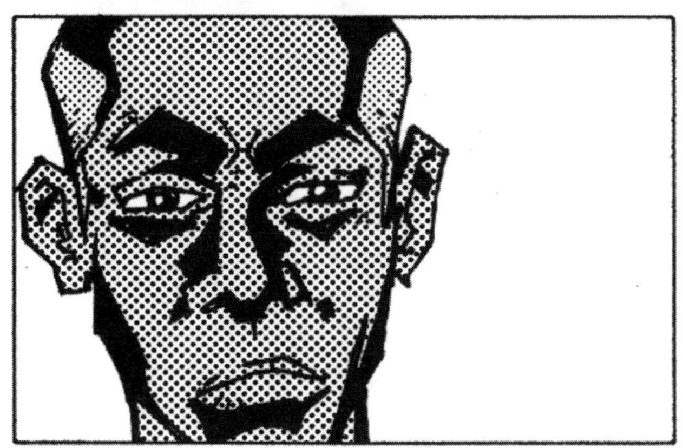

YES. OK...
BUT...

I GOT INTO THE ACCOUNTING DATABASE AT MIDAS LAST NIGHT. I BET I CAN PROVE SOME ILL STUFF IS GOING DOWN IN THERE.

WELL, YOU KNOW, I'M JUST SAYING IT COULD BE IMPORTANT...
...HERE YOU GO, CASTRUCCIO...
...MORE IMPORTANT THAN AP EURO, NAHMEAN?
HOP

I DON'T KNOW ABOUT THAT... SCHOOL IS GONNA GET YOU THAT EDGE. THEN WE CAN GO LEGIT AND MAKE SOME REAL MONEY.

MAMMON BOUGHT BIT BANK FOR 1.5 BILLION DOLLARS. 1.5 BILLION DOLLARS WOULD SOLVE A LOT OF PROBLEMS
RICH PEOPLE HAVE PROBLEMS TOO, THEO.
TAT'S TAT

I WANT THEM PROBLEMS.

WHATEVER...SCHOOL IS SOME BULLSHIT AND YOU KNOW IT!

FORTUNE SHOWS HER POWER WHERE VALOR HAS NOT PREPARED TO RESIST HER...
MA?
...AND TURNS HER FORCES WHERE SHE KNOWS DEFENSES HAVE NOT BEEN RAISED.
MA?
AND THE PRINCE WHO RELIES ENTIRELY ON FORTUNE IS LOST...
...WHEN IT CHANGES.

A PRINCE IS RESPECTED WHEN HE IS EITHER A TRUE FRIEND OR A DOWNRIGHT ENEMY.

WOAHHHH!

COOL!

NO! I CAN'T EVEN LEAVE THE GOTTDAMN HOUSE.

BECAUSE IF TWO OF YOUR POWERFUL NEIGHBORS COME TO BLOWS, IF ONE OF THEM CONQUERS, YOU HAVE EITHER TO FEAR HIM OR NOT.

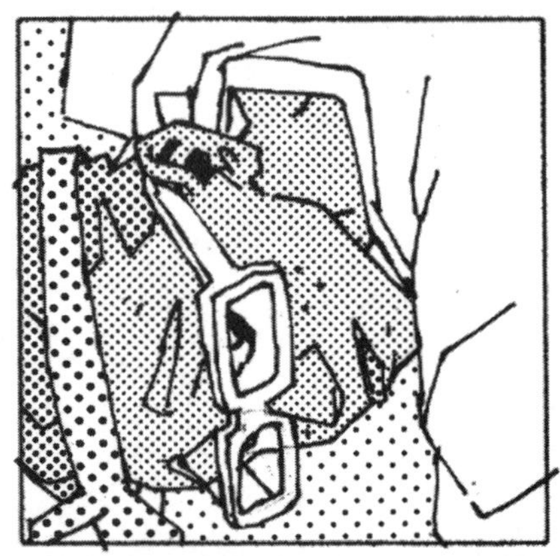

HE WHO CONQUERS DOES NOT WANT FRIENDS WHO WILL NOT AID HIM IN THE TIME OF TRIAL...

...HE WHO LOSES WILL NOT HARBOUR YOU BECAUSE YOU DID NOT WILLINGLY, SWORD IN HAND, COURT HIS FATE.

ALTHOUGH A PRINCE MAY RISE FROM A PRIVATE STATION IN TWO WAYS–WICKEDNESS OR FAVOR OF THE PEOPLE–NEITHER OF WHICH CAN BE ENTIRELY ATTRIBUTED TO FORTUNE OR GENIUS.

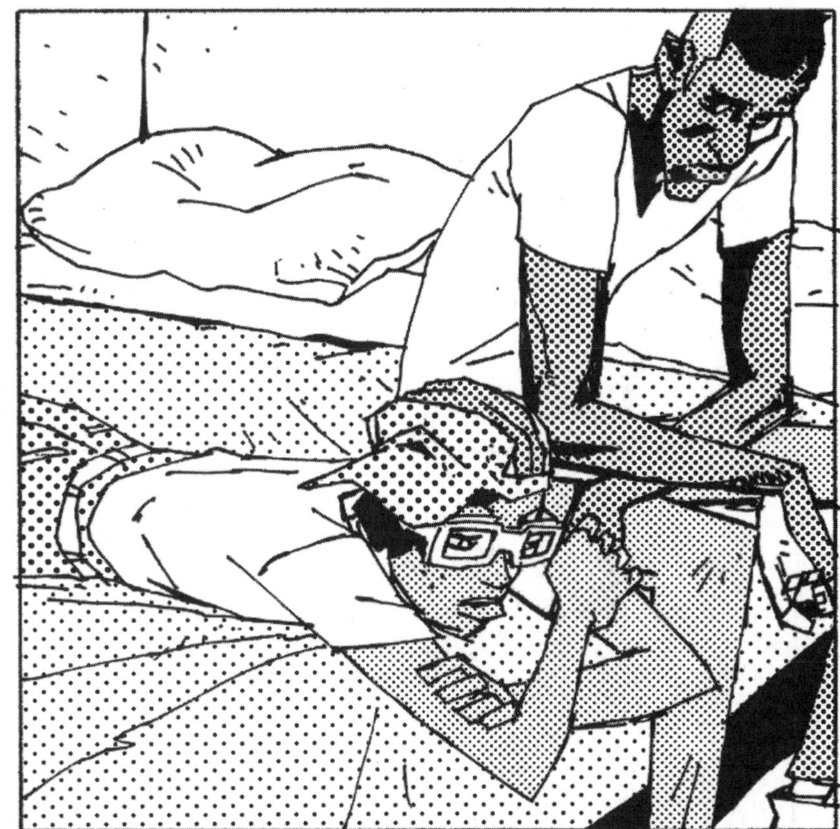

ABOVE ALL, A PRINCE MUST LIVE AMONGST HIS PEOPLE IN SUCH A WAY THAT NO UNEXPECTED CIRCUMSTANCE–WHETHER GOOD OR ILL–SHALL MAKE HIM CHANGE.

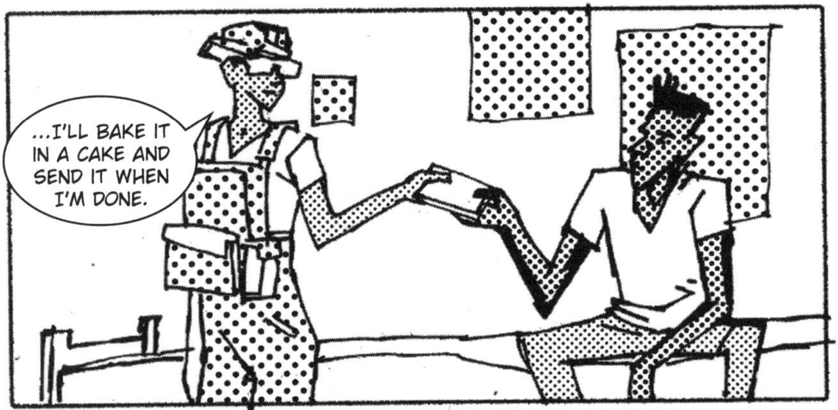

A WISE MAN OUGHT ALWAYS TO FOLLOW THE PATHS BEATEN BY GREAT MEN, AND TO IMITATE THOSE WHO HAVE BEEN SUPREME, SO THAT IF HIS ABILITY DOES NOT EQUAL THEIRS, AT LEAST IT WILL SAVOR OF IT.

ARE FORTRESSES, AND MANY OTHER THINGS TO WHICH PRINCES OFTEN RESORT,

ADVANTAGEOUS OR HURTFUL?

BUT TO COME TO THOSE WHO, BY THEIR OWN ABILITY AND NOT THROUGH FORTUNE, HAVE RISEN TO BE PRINCES...

...I SAY THAT MOSES, CYRUS, ROMULUS, THESEUS, AND SUCH LIKE ARE THE MOST EXCELLENT EXAMPLES...
UNIVERSIT

...AND IN EXAMINING THEIR ACTIONS AND LIVES ONE CANNOT SEE THAT THEY OWED ANYTHING TO FORTUNE...

ZZZZ

...BEYOND OPPORTUNITY, WHICH BROUGHT THEM THE MATERIAL TO MOLD INTO THE FORM WHICH SEEMED BEST TO THEM.
OFFICE of the BURSAR

A WISE PRINCE, WHEN HE HAS THE OPPORTUNITY...
YOU'RE IN MY SEAT, PUNK!

...OUGHT WITH CRAFT TO FOSTER SOME ANIMOSITY AGAINST HIMSELF, SO THAT, HAVING CRUSHED IT, HIS RENOWN MAY RISE HIGHER.
SOK!

WELL, YOU COULD APPLY FOR ONE OF MAMMON BANK'S DEFERRED EDUCATION LOANS.
WITHOUT THAT OPPORTUNITY THEIR POWERS OF MIND WOULD HAVE BEEN EXTINGUISHED...

...AND WITHOUT THOSE POWERS THE OPPORTUNITY WOULD HAVE COME IN VAIN.
PRINCES BECOME GREAT WHEN THEY OVERCOME THE DIFFICULTIES AND OBSTACLES BEFORE THEM.
NOTHING MAKES A PRINCE MORE ESTEEMED AS GREAT ENTERPRISES AND SETTING A FINE EXAMPLE.
SOME PRINCES DISARM THEIR SUBJECTS. OTHERS KEEP THEIR SUBJECTS DISTRACTED BY FACTIONS.
SOME HAVE BUILT FORTRESSES, WHILE OTHERS HAVE OVERTHROWN AND DESTROYED THEM.

THERE NEVER WAS A NEW PRINCE WHO HAS DISARMED HIS SUBJECTS.

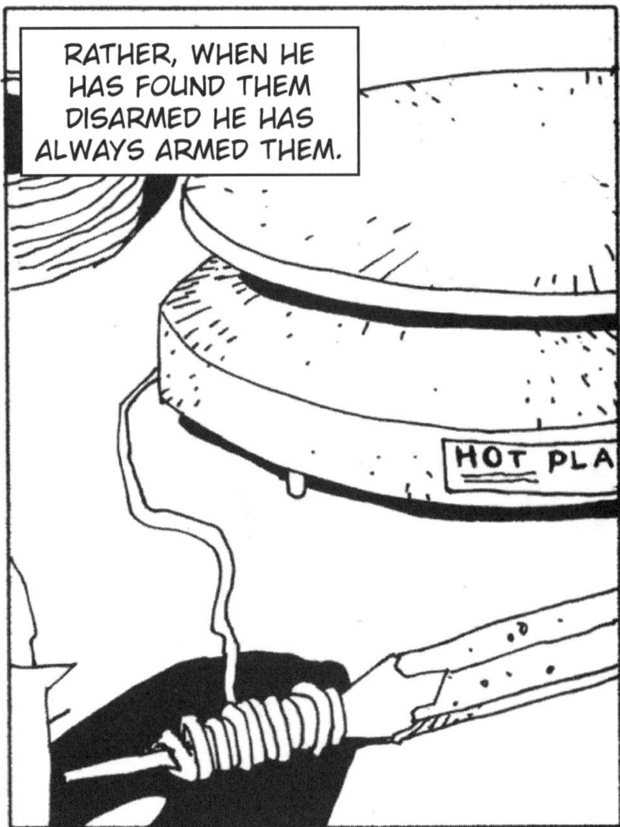
RATHER, WHEN HE HAS FOUND THEM DISARMED HE HAS ALWAYS ARMED THEM.
HOT PLA

BY ARMING THEM, THOSE ARMS BECOME YOURS.
THOSE WHO WERE DISTRUSTED BECOME FAITHFUL.

THOSE WHO WERE FAITHFUL ARE KEPT SO.
YOUR SUBJECTS BECOME YOUR ADHERENTS.

VOL CLMV

# Incarcerated Youth Exposes Private Juvenile Detention Fraud

**From inside Labyrinth Detention Center in Buffalo,New York, teenager Theodore Morton shed light on the fraudulent collusion between a local judge and a private contractor.**

by Ed Burke

Although Theodore Morton, 18, was no ... at the tender age of 15, he was ... Crete on charges

Although Theodore Theodore, 18, was no angel when, at the tender age of 15, he was brought before Judge Jonathan Crete on charges of identity theft and larceny authorities now agree that the sentence he received was far too harsh for a first time juvenile offender. And Theodore wasn't the only youth unjustly sentenced to harsh terms at Labyrinth Detention Center.

... authorities now agree ... sentence he received was far too harsh for a first time juvenile offender. And Theodore wasn't the only youth unjustly sentenced to harsh terms at Labyrinth Detention Center.

It all would've gone unnoticed if not for the ingenuity of Theodore, who combined ordinary and contraband items to create a computer and uncover incriminating evidence connecting Judge Jonathan Crete and Contractor Milton Daedelus.

With just a cell phone and a game box Theodore hacked into the Daedelus records and the personal mail accounts of Mr. Crete and Mr. Daedelus and then sent digital and hand written hard copies of emails, receipts and other evidence as well as an appeal on his and the other interned at Labyrinth to ...he District Attorney's office. While his ingenuity ...as been applauded and has triggered an investiga...n on underhanded dealings, Theodore' craft has ...sed a bit of a conundrum for authorities. ...rict Attorney, Maurine Davis had this to say, ...hough I cannot fully condone Mr. Theodore' ...ior, it goes without saying that his ingenuity ...nning serves for the better good of himself ... fellow inmates." As for now Theodore's ...d those of his fellow inmates have been ...ut. When asked about his means, Theo...nded, "...because how ...

NEVER WAS ANYTHING GREAT ACHIEVED WITHOUT DANGER.

CONCERNING NEW PRINCIPALITIES...

...WHICH ARE ACQUIRED BY ONE'S OWN ARMS AND ABILITY.

BECOMING A PRINCE FROM A PRIVATE STATION PRESUPPOSES EITHER ABILITY OR FORTUNE...

...ONE OR THE OTHER OF THESE THINGS WILL MITIGATE MANY DIFFICULTIES.

RUN DMC

COFFEE?

THE CHOICE OF SERVANTS IS OF NO LITTLE IMPORTANCE TO A PRINCE.

THEY ARE GOOD OR NOT ACCORDING TO THE DISCRIMINATION OF THE PRINCE.

KEEP YOUR RECEIPTS!

THE FIRST OPINION WHICH ONE FORMS OF A PRINCE, AND OF HIS UNDERSTANDING IS BY OBSERVING THE MEN HE HAS AROUND HIM.

I'M SORRY...

...BUT WE CANNOT
APPROVE YOUR BUSINESS
LOAN AT THE MOMENT.

LOOKS LIKE YOU'VE
GOT SOME OUTSTANDING
SCHOOL LOANS.

THOSE WHO BY VALOROUS WAYS BECOME PRINCES...

...LIKE THESE MEN...

...ACQUIRE A PRINCIPALITY WITH DIFFICULTY...

...BUT THEY KEEP IT WITH EASE.

THE DIFFICULTIES THEY HAVE IN ACQUIRING IT RISE IN PART FROM THE NEW RULES AND METHODS WHICH THEY ARE FORCED TO INTRODUCE TO ESTABLISH THEIR GOVERNMENT AND ITS SECURITY...

...AND IT OUGHT TO BE REMEMBERED THAT THERE IS NOTHING MORE DIFFICULT TO TAKE IN HAND, MORE PERILOUS TO CONDUCT, OR MORE UNCERTAIN IN ITS SUCCESS, THAN TO TAKE THE LEAD IN THE INTRODUCTION OF A NEW ORDER OF THINGS...

...BECAUSE THE INNOVATOR HAS FOR ENEMIES ALL THOSE WHO HAVE DONE WELL UNDER THE OLD CONDITIONS...

...AND LUKEWARM DEFENDERS IN THOSE WHO MAY DO WELL UNDER THE NEW.

# CONCERNING A CIVIL PRINCIPALITY

GENIUS OR FORTUNE AREN'T ALTOGETHER NECESSARY TO ATTAIN TO IT, BUT RATHER A HAPPY SHREWDNESS.

THESE PRINCIPALITIES ARE LIABLE TO DANGER WHEN THEY ARE PASSING FROM THE CIVIL TO THE ABSOLUTE ORDER OF GOVERNMENT, FOR SUCH PRINCES EITHER RULE PERSONALLY OR THROUGH MAGISTRATES.

IT IS NECESSARY, THEREFORE, IF WE DESIRE TO DISCUSS THIS MATTER THOROUGHLY, TO INQUIRE WHETHER THESE INNOVATORS CAN RELY ON THEMSELVES...

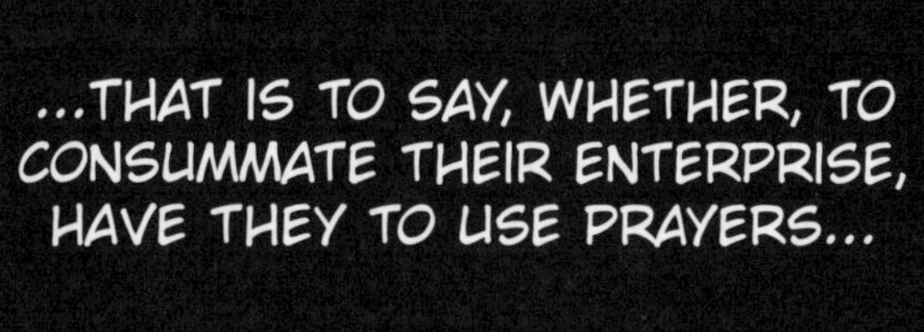

HENCE IT IS THAT ALL ARMED PROPHETS HAVE CONQUERED, AND THE UNARMED ONES HAVE BEEN DESTROYED.

...BUT IN TROUBLED TIMES, WHEN THE STATE HAS NEED OF ITS CITIZENS, THEN HE FINDS BUT FEW.

Economics
Overnight Oliga
New Money Ne
Influence?
Mending the net:
ost Pop Punk's innovation
tech and business
ctices
w Flatterers
uld be avoided:
prince ought to hold
course by choosing
e men in his state,
ng to them only the
speaking the truth
$3.14
AUGUST 11

Mending the net:
Post Pop Punk's innovation
in tech and business
practices
How Flatterers
should be avoided:
A wise prince ought to hold
a third course by choosing
the wise men in his state,
and giving to them only the
liberty of speaking the truth
to him.

Economics
Overnight Oligarchy:
New Money New
Influence?
$3.14
AUGUST 11, 2009

WES

HONK!
HONK

CONCERNING NEW PRINCIPALITIES WHICH ARE ACQUIRED...

...EITHER BY THE ARMS OF OTHERS OR BY GOOD FORTUNE

HEY, I'VE AN APPOINTMENT WITH ROXANNE AT SIX.
HI!
SURE THING. ONE MOMENT.

...OK, THEN I'LL SEND HIM BACK.

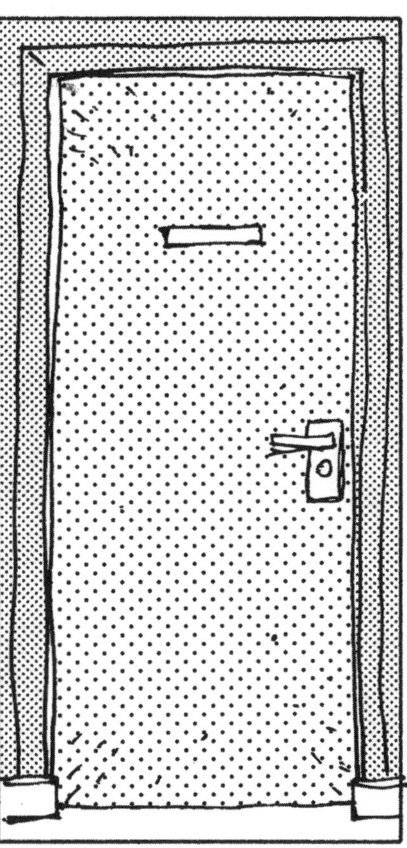

I HAVE ANOTHER YOUNG MAN HERE TO SEE YOU, ROXANNE.
UH...

STATES THAT RISE UNEXPECTEDLY, LIKE ALL OTHER THINGS IN NATURE THAT RISE AND GROW RAPIDLY...

...CANNOT LEAVE THEIR FOUNDATIONS FIXED IN SUCH A WAY THAT THE FIRST STORM WILL. OVERTHROW THEM.
OK, SEND HIM IN.

THE PRINCES MUST BE PREPARED TO HOLD THE FORTUNE THAT HAS BEEN THROWN INTO THEIR LAPS.

?

ROXIE!
YIP YIP

THE FOUNDATIONS OTHERS HAVE LAID BEFORE THEY BECAME PRINCES...
THEO!

WHAT THE FUCK?!

YEAH!

...THE UNEXPECTEDLY PRINCE MUST LAY AFTERWARDS.

IF THE MAN BE RICH LET HIM EAT WHEN HE IS HUNGRY; IF HE BE POOR, THEN WHEN HE CAN...
I'M SAYIN'...

...WHY EVEN HAVE A RED MENU?
-WOAH!

WHAT?

YOU CAN'T SMOKE IN HERE!

I CAN'T SMOKE IN HERE?!

NOPE

SORRY, SIR. YOU CAN'T SMOKE HERE.

THIS IS A PUBLIC RESTAURANT.

THIS IS A PUBLIC RESTAURANT...
...WHERE HAVE YOU BEEN?

SIR-
I'M PUTTING IT OUT! GOTTDAMN!

KSHHHH

SO...
WHAT ARE YOU DOING FOR WORK?

WELL ...THAT'S WHY I WAS COMING TO SEE YOU.

OF COURSE, OF COURSE... IT'D BE LIKE OLD TIMES.

HA HA HA HA HA HA HA HA HA HA HA HA HA HA

THOSE WHO SOLELY BY GOOD FORTUNE BECOME PRINCES FROM BEING PRIVATE HAVE LITTLE TROUBLE IN RISING...

...BUT MUCH IN KEEPING ATOP.

HA HA HA HA HA HA
HA HA HA HA HA HA HA

JOHNNY?

DIDN'T EXPECT TO SEE YOU HERE. I HAVEN'T SEEN YOU IN YEARS... NOT SINCE-

THE TRIAL.

HEHEHE.

NO HARD FEELINGS, KIRBY?

NO, NOT AT ALL. LIKEWISE, I HOPE... WHAT ARE YOU DOING HERE?

HERE WITH A FRIEND...
...FROM WORK.

WELL...

YOU'RE STILL AT MAMMON, RIGHT?
GIVE ME A CALL SOMETIME.

THEODORE... ABSOLUTELY, PLEASE, TAKE MINE.

NO NEED.

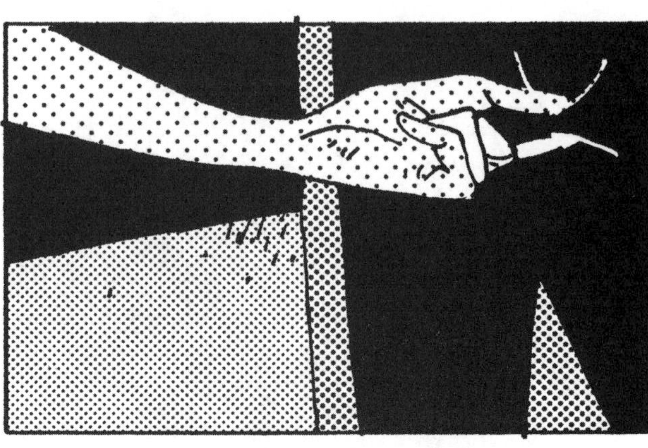

WHO WAS THAT?
HMMM...
...YOU'RE DRUNK?! HAHA!
A LITTLE

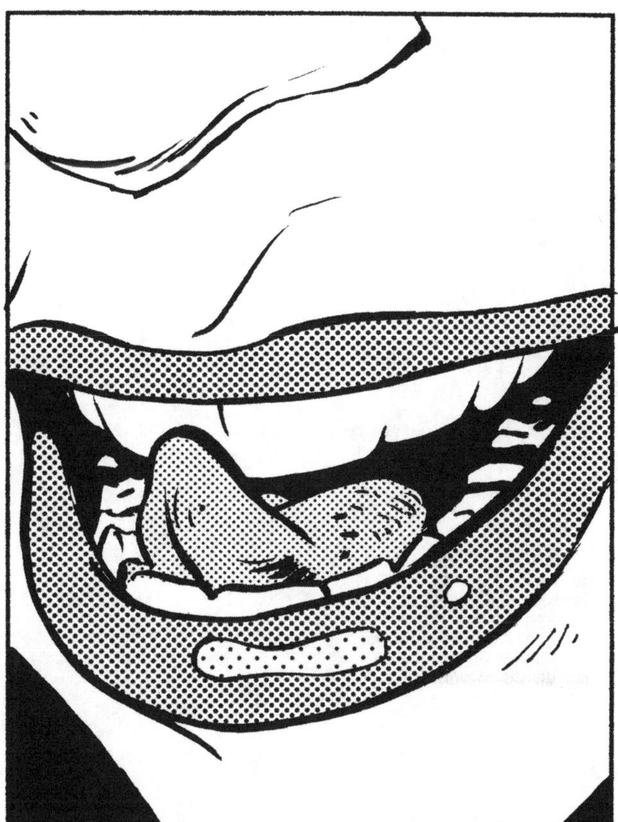

LET'S GO...

## CONCERNING CRUELTY AND CLEMENCY, AND WHETHER IT IS BETTER TO BE LOVED THAN FEARED.

IT IS NECESSARY FOR A PRINCE WISHING TO HOLD HIS OWN TO KNOW HOW TO DO WRONG AND TO MAKE USE OF IT OR NOT ACCORDING TO NECESSITY.

I MUST NOT FAIL TO WARN A PRINCE, WHO BY MEANS OF SECRET FAVORS HAS ACQUIRED A NEW STATE, THAT HE MUST WELL CONSIDER THE REASONS WHICH INDUCED THOSE TO FAVOR HIM WHO DID SO.

AND IF IT BE NOT A NATURAL AFFECTION TOWARDS HIM, BUT ONLY DISCONTENT WITH THEIR GOVERNMENT, THEN HE WILL ONLY KEEP THEM FRIENDLY WITH GREAT TROUBLE AND DIFFICULTY, FOR IT WILL BE IMPOSSIBLE TO SATISFY.

AND WEIGHING EXAMPLES FROM ANCIENT AND MODERN AFFAIRS, WE SHALL FIND IT IS EASIER FOR THE PRINCE TO MAKE FRIENDS OF THOSE MEN WHO WERE CONTENTED UNDER THE FORMER GOVERNMENT, AND ARE THEREFORE HIS ENEMIES.

SO WHAT DO YOU GUYS THINK ABOUT THE MAMMON OFFER?
MAMMON OFFER?

CHAKA
CHAKA
CHAKA

CHAKA
CHAKA
CHAKA

NESS

day, October 13, 2011

# Mammon Buys Mumble Bunny

Tech giant scores with hostile takeover of small yet promising social

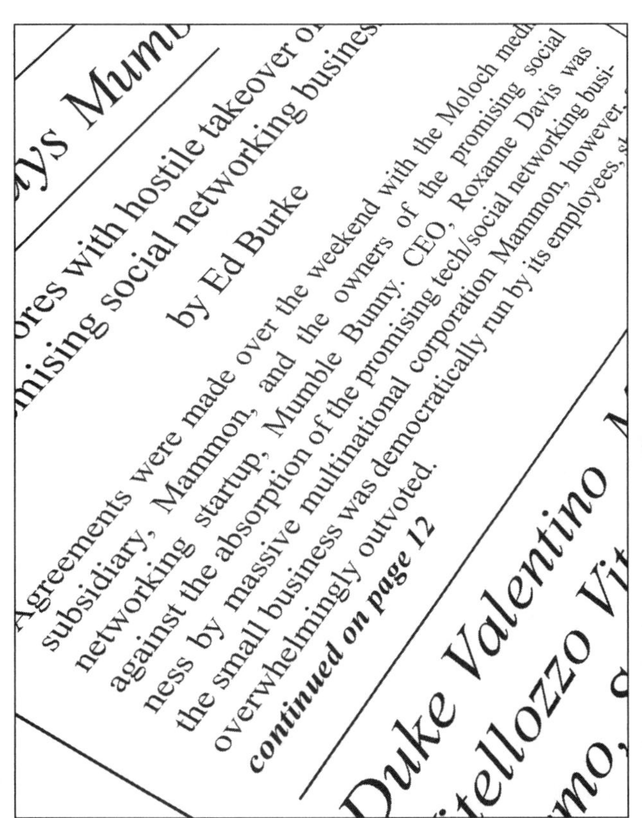

ys Mum

ores with hostile takeover o
mising social networking busines

by Ed Burke

Agreements were made over the weekend with the Moloch media subsidiary, Mammon, and the owners of the promising social networking startup, Mumble Bunny. CEO, Roxanne Davis was against the absorption of the promising tech/social networking business by massive multinational corporation Mammon, however, the small business was democratically run by its employees, s overwhelmingly outvoted.

***continued on page 12***

Duke Valentino

itellozzo Vit

mo,

contender in the Social Networking game. Mumble Bunny set it apart from its competitors with its attractive and intuitive interface and addictive recruitment campaigns. It remains to be seen however if the staff will survive the disolving of the democratic structure. Theodore Windfall, Chief of Marketing at Mumble Bunny, finds himself in a cush new position within Corporate Mammon, taking the reigns as VP of Software from Kirby Cunningham.

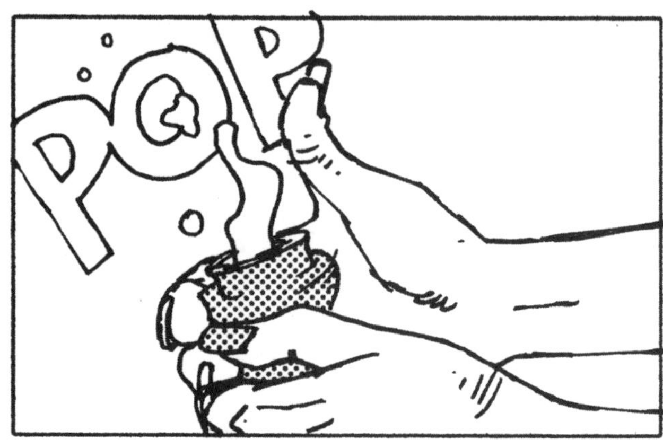

HE WHO DOES OTHERWISE, EITHER FROM TIMIDITY OR EVIL ADVICE, IS ALWAYS COMPELLED TO KEEP THE KNIFE IN HIS HAND...

...NEITHER CAN HE RELY ON HIS SUBJECTS, NOR CAN THEY ATTACH THEMSELVES TO HIM.

NEVER IMAGINE THAT ONE CAN CHOOSE A PERFECTLY SAFE COURSE; RATHER, EXPECT TO HAVE TO TAKE DOUBTFUL ONES.

WELL, BILLIE HAD IT COMING, BUT ROXANNE?

YOU THINK IF SHE KNEW, ROXANNE WOULD'VE EVER HIRED HIM?

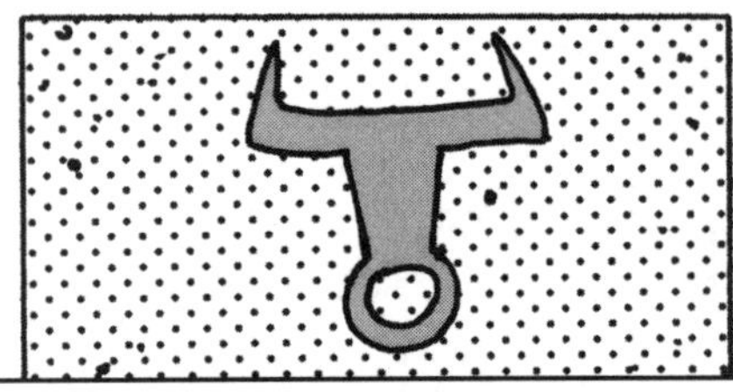

PRINCES BECOME GREAT WHEN THEY OVERCOME THE OBSTACLES BY WHICH THEY ARE CONFRONTED...

*New Management at Moloch*

Moloch's Media branch, Mammon, gets a big change in management. New young prince, Theodore Windfall, takes position at the top

By Ed Burke

...AND THEREFORE FORTUNE, WHEN SHE DESIRES TO MAKE A NEW PRINCE GREAT, CAUSES ENEMIES TO ARISE AND FORM DESIGNS AGAINST HIM.

OBSTACLES ARISE IN FRONT OF A PRINCE IN ORDER THAT HE MAY HAVE THE OPPORTUNITY OF OVERCOMING THEM, AND BY THEM TO MOUNT HIGHER...

...AS BY A LADDER WHICH HIS ENEMIES HAVE RAISED.

VOL CLMIIV

New York, Tuesday

*New Beginnings to Place Old Friends at Odds*

Ex Mumble Bunny CEO starts Nonprofit Corporate Watch Dog Organization

By Charles Montesquieu

I met Roxanne de Beauvoir outside of Moloch headquarters on Broadway on Monday. She stood in front of a inflammable ocean of picket signs shouting sparks

FOR THIS REASON MANY CONSIDER THAT A WISE PRINCE OUGHT TO FOSTER SOME ANIMOSITY AGAINST HIMSELF SO THAT, HAVING CRUSHED IT, HIS RENOWN MAY RISE HIGHER.

YET IT CANNOT BE CALLED TALENT TO SLAY FELLOW CITIZENS, TO DECEIVE FRIENDS, TO BE WITHOUT FAITH, WITHOUT MERCY; SUCH METHODS MAY GAIN EMPIRE, BUT...

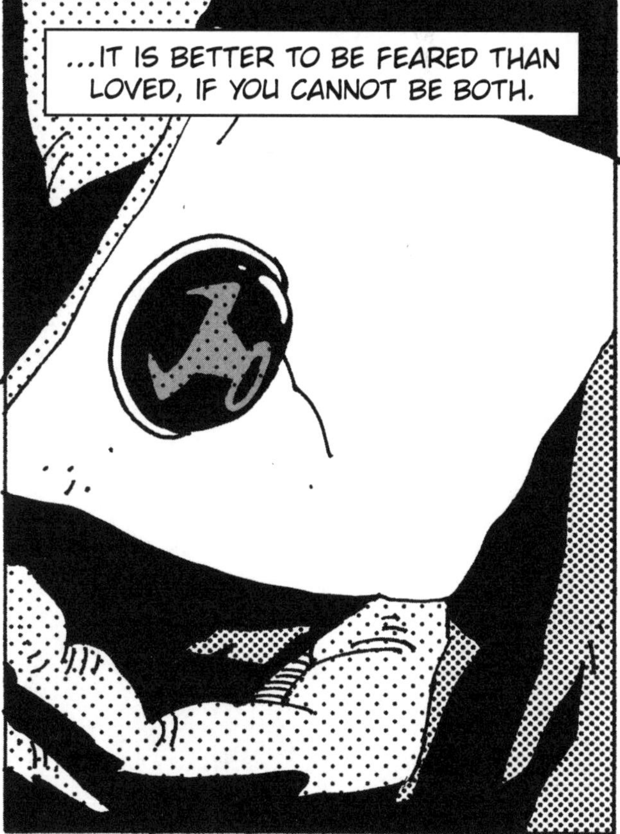

# About the Author

Niccolo Machiavelli
*(May 3, 1469 – June 21, 1527)*

was an Italian philosopher and one of the main founders of modern political science.
He is best known for Il Principe (The Prince); a manifestation for gaining and keeping power.
(source: Wikipedia).

# Other titles from SmarterComics[tm]

**EAT THAT FROG!**
**from SmarterComics**

by Brian Tracy

Procrastinators, be advised: Success is not a magical combination of genetics and fashion sense. Rather, it is a series of time management behaviors which must be practiced on a regular basis. Luckily, "EAT THAT FROG!" will show you how to deal with those challenging tasks you keep putting off in an accessible comic book format.

**THE ART OF WAR from SmarterComics**

by Sun Tzu

Written by an ancient Chinese military general and philosopher, THE ART OF WAR reveals the subtle secrets of successful competition – equally applicable to war, business, politics, sports, law, poker, gaming, and life. Required reading in modern business schools!

**THE LAW OF ATTRACTION from SmarterComics**

by D.J. Coffman

Love, happiness, health, wealth? No matter what you desire, „The Law of Attraction" from SmarterComics is the ultimate guide to attracting ANYTHING you want in your life. Successful people have been deliberately using this „Law" for over a century to amass great fortunes and achieve their dreams.

**OVERACHIEVEMENT from SmarterComics**

by Dr. John Eliot

In OVERACHIEVEMENT from SmarterComics, Dr. Eliot offers the rest of us the unconventional and counterintuitive concepts embraced by Olympic athletes, business moguls, rock stars, top surgeons, salespeople, and financial experts who have turned to him for performance-enhancement advice.

## Other titles from SmarterComics™

**THE 80/20 PRINCIPLE from SmarterComics**

by Richard Koch

Learn the time-tested secret of achieving more with less using "the 80/20 Principle." Based on the counter-intuitive fact that 80% of results flow from 20% of causes, it is the guiding principle of highly effective people and organizations.

**FORTUNE FAVORS THE BOLD from SmarterComics**

by Franco Arda

Written by the founder of SmarterComics, this powerful little manual packs a punch. If you want to grab life by the horns but tend to drag your feet doing it, this comic is for you.

**THINK & GROW RICH from SmarterComics**

by Napoleon Hill

Want to learn the principles of getting rich in less than an hour? Take the illustrated advice of millionaire Andrew Carnegie, whose observations make up the heart of the best-selling classic "Think and Grow Rich." Now updated into an engaging comic book format, you can quickly glean Carnegie's wisdom from these beautifully illustrated panels.

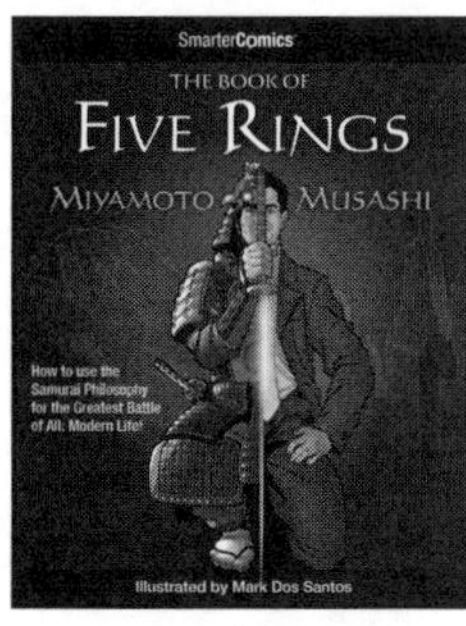


**THE BOOK OF 5 RINGS from SmarterComics**

by Miyamoto Musashi

Infamous 17th century samurai Miyamoto Musashi (1584-1645) never lost a fight. His unprecedented winning streak wasn't based on supernatural powers: he was a keen master of strategy, timing, and the nuances of human interaction. He recorded his brilliant observations in „The Book of Five Rings" in 1643.

# QUIZ

*Please visit www.smartercomics.com/quizzes for the answers and more quizzes.*

1. **All powers that have rule over men are…**

    a) Wealthy.

    b) Inherently corrupt.

    c) Principalities.

2. **He who conquers does not want…**

    a) Friends who will not aid him in a time of trial.

    b) To deal with the day-to-day minutiae of rule.

    c) Servants who are willing to court his fate with sword in hand.

3. **A wise man should understand the paths beaten by great men, and…**

    a) Forge one's own path to greatness.

    b) Take credit for the success of others.

    c) Imitate those who have been successful.

4. **Becoming a prince from a private station presupposes…**

    a) Betrayal at one time or another.

    b) Either ability or fortune.

    c) The support of the people.

5. **According to the discrimination of the prince, servants are…**

    a) Either good or not.

    b) Paid well for their services.

    c) Working against the prince.

**6. What is necessary to attain a civil principality?**

a) Genius.

b) Shrewdness.

c) Fortune.

**7. What is the greatest challenge for those who become princes by good fortune?**

a) Losing focus.

b) Rising to power.

c) Staying in power.

**8. A prince wishing to hold his own must know how to do wrong and…**

a) Avoid its use for the betterment of the principality.

b) Create laws and regulations to limit such wrongdoing.

c) Make use of it or not according to necessity.

**9. Prudence consists of…**

a) Distinguishing the character of trouble.

b) Choosing the lesser of two evils.

c) Both of the above.

**10. Fortune, when she desires to make a prince great…**

a) Causes a strong ambition to burn within his heart.

b) Causes enemies to arise and form designs against him.

c) Causes friends and allies to flock to his side.

the
Prince
available for
iPhone, iPad,
Android & Kindle
SmarterComics
MACHIAVELLI
the
Prince
AN ILLUSTRATED TALE OF
POWER, BETRAYAL, AND REV

www.smartercomics.com